Python:

The Ultimate Beginner's Guide

Lee Maxwell

© 2016

TABLE OF CONTENT

Introduction

I want to thank you and congratulate you for downloading the book, "Python: The Ultimate Beginner's Guide".

This book contains proven steps and strategies on Python: The Ultimate Beginner's Guide...

More than six years prior, in December 1989, I was searching for a "pastime" programming venture that would keep me involved amid the week around Christmas. My office ... would be shut, yet I had a home PC, and very little else staring me in the face. I chose to compose a mediator for the new scripting dialect I had been pondering recently: a relative of ABC that would speak to Unix/C programmers. I picked Python as a working title for the venture, being in a somewhat flippant disposition (and a major fanatic of Monty Python's Flying Circus).

Python 2.0 was discharged on 16 October 2000 and had many major new components, including a cycle-recognizing city worker and support for Unicode. With this discharge the improvement procedure was changed and turned out to be more straightforward and group upheld.

Python 3.0 (which right off the bat in its advancement was generally alluded to as Python 3000 or py3k), a noteworthy, in reverse contradictory discharge, was discharged on 3 December 2008 after a long stretch of testing. A hefty portion of its real elements have been backported to the retrogressive perfect Python 2.6.x and 2.7.x form arrangement.

Thanks again for downloading this book, I hope you enjoy it!

Chapter 1

Python

Python was imagined in the late 1980s, and its execution started in December 1989 by Guido van Rossum at Centrum Wiskunde and Informatica (CWI) in the Netherlands as a successor to the ABC dialect (itself motivated by SETL) fit for exemption taking care of and interfacing with the working framework Amoeba. Van Rossum is Python's key creator, and his proceeding with focal part in choosing the heading of Python is reflected in the title given to him by the Python people group, big-hearted tyrant forever (BDFL).

About the inception of Python, Van Rossum wrote in 1996.

More than six years prior, in December 1989, I was searching for a "pastime" programming venture that would keep me involved amid the week around

Christmas. My office ... would be shut, yet I had a home PC, and very little else staring me in the face. I chose to compose a mediator for the new scripting dialect I had been pondering recently: a relative of ABC that would speak to Unix/C programmers. I picked Python as a working title for the venture, being in a somewhat flippant disposition (and a major fanatic of Monty Python's Flying Circus).

Python 2.0 was discharged on 16 October 2000 and had many major new components, including a cycle-recognizing city worker and support for Unicode. With this discharge the improvement procedure was changed and turned out to be more straightforward and group upheld.

Python 3.0 (which right off the bat in its advancement was generally alluded to as Python 3000 or py3k), a noteworthy, in reverse contradictory discharge, was discharged on 3 December 2008 after a long stretch of testing. A hefty portion of its real elements have been backported to the retrogressive perfect Python 2.6.x and 2.7.x form arrangement.

Elements and rationality

Python is a multi-worldview programming dialect: question arranged programming and organized writing computer programs are completely upheld, and numerous dialect highlights bolster practical programming and viewpoint situated programming (counting by metaprogramming and metaobjects (enchantment strategies)). Numerous different ideal models are bolstered by means of augmentations, including configuration by contract and rationale programming.

Python utilizes dynamic writing and a blend of reference numbering and a cycle-recognizing trash specialist for memory administration. An essential element of Python is powerful name determination (late official), which ties technique and variable names amid program execution.

The outline of Python offers some support for utilitarian programming in the Lisp custom. The dialect has delineate() and channel() capacities; list appreciations, word references, and sets; and generator expressions. The standard library has two modules (itertools and functools) that execute utilitarian devices acquired from Haskell and Standard ML.

The center logic of the dialect is outlined by the report The Zen of Python (PEP 20), which incorporates adages, for example,

- Beautiful is superior to terrible

- Explicit is superior to verifiable

- Simple is superior to complex

- Complex is superior to confused

- Readability checks

As opposed to requiring all coveted usefulness to be incorporated with the dialect's center, Python was intended to be very extensible. Python can likewise be inserted in existing applications that need a programmable interface. This plan of a little center dialect with a vast standard library and an effectively extensible translator was planned by Van Rossum from the begin due to his dissatisfactions with ABC, which upheld the inverse attitude.

While offering decision in coding approach, the Python logic rejects rich language structure, for example, in Perl, for a sparser, less-messed syntax. As Alex Martelli put it: "To depict something as astute is not viewed as a compliment in the Python culture." Python's reasoning rejects the Perl "there is more than one approach to do it" way to deal with dialect configuration for "there ought to be one—and ideally just a single—evident approach to do it".

Python's engineers endeavor to keep away from untimely enhancement, and besides, dismiss patches to non-basic parts of CPython that would offer a minimal increment in speed at the cost of clarity. At the point when speed is imperative, a Python developer can move time-basic capacities to expansion modules written in dialects, for example, C, or take a stab at utilizing PyPy, an in the nick of time compiler. Cython is additionally accessible, which makes an interpretation of a Python script into C and makes coordinate C-level API calls into the Python translator.

A vital objective of Python's designers is making it amusing to utilize. This is reflected in the birthplace of the name, which originates from Monty Python, and in an every so often energetic way to deal with instructional exercises and reference materials, for example, utilizing cases that allude to spam and eggs rather than the standard foo and bar.

A typical neologism in the Python people group is pythonic, which can have an extensive variety of implications identified with program style. To state that code is pythonic is to state that it utilizes Python colloquialisms well, that it is normal or shows familiarity with the dialect, that it adjusts with Python's moderate logic and accentuation on decipherability. Conversely, code that is hard to comprehend or peruses like an unpleasant translation from another programming dialect is called unpythonic.

Clients and admirers of Python, particularly those considered proficient or experienced, are regularly alluded to as Pythonists, Pythonistas, and Pythoneers.

Punctuation and semantics

Python punctuation and semantics

Python is planned to be a profoundly decipherable dialect. It is intended to have an uncluttered visual format, frequently utilizing English watchwords where different dialects utilize accentuation. Promote, Python has less syntactic exemptions and unique cases than C or Pascal.

Space

Python sentence structure and semantics
§ Indentation

Python utilizes whitespace space to delimit pieces - as opposed to wavy props or catchphrases. An expansion in space comes after specific proclamations; a lessening in space means the end of the present piece. This component is additionally once in a while named the off-side run the show.

Chapter 2

Explanations and control stream

Python's announcements incorporate (among others):

• The task explanation (token '=', the equivalents sign). This works uniquely in contrast to in conventional basic programming dialects, and this principal system (counting the way of Python's form of factors) lights up numerous different elements of the dialect. Task in C, e.g., x = 2, means "wrote variable name x gets a duplicate of numeric esteem 2". The (right-hand) esteem is duplicated into an apportioned stockpiling area for which the (left-hand) variable name is the typical address. The memory allotted to the variable is sufficiently huge (possibly very huge) for the pronounced sort. In the least complex instance of Python task, utilizing a similar illustration, x = 2, means "(nonexclusive) name x gets a reference to a different, progressively apportioned protest of numeric (int) kind of significant worth 2." This is named restricting the name to the *q*uestion. Since the name's stockpiling area doesn't contain the demonstrated esteem, it is despicable to call it a variable. Names might be in this manner bounce back whenever to objects of incredibly fluctuating sorts, including strings, techni*q*ues, complex items with information and strategies, and so forth. Progressive assignments of a typical esteem to different names, e.g., x = 2; y = 2; z = 2 bring about apportioning stockpiling to (at most) three names and one numeric *q*uestion, to which each of the three names are bound. Since a name is a non specific reference holder it is preposterous to relate a settled information sort with it. However at a given time a name will be bound to some *q*uestion, which will have a sort; in this manner there is changing writing.

• The if articulation, which restrictively executes a piece of code, alongside else and elif (a withdrawal of else-if).

• The for articulation, which emphasizes over an iterable protest, catching every component to a neighborhood variable for use by the connected square.

• The while proclamation, which executes a piece of code the length of its condition is valid.

• The attempt explanation, which permits special cases brought up in its appended code square to be gotten and took care of by with the exception of provisos; it likewise guarantees that tidy up code in an at last piece will dependably be run paying little heed to how the square exits.

• The class proclamation, which executes a square of code and joins its nearby namespace to a class, for use in question situated programming.

• The def explanation, which characterizes a capacity or technique.

• The with explanation (from Python 2.5), which encases a code hinder inside a setting director (for instance, securing a bolt before the square of code is run and discharging the bolt thereafter, or opening a record and afterward shutting it), permitting Resource Acquisition Is Initialization (RAII)- like conduct.

• The pass explanation, which serves as a NOP. It is grammatically expected to make a void code square.

• The declare explanation, utilized amid investigating to check for conditions that should apply.

• The yield articulation, which gives back an esteem from a generator work. From Python 2.5, yield is likewise an administrator. This shape is utilized to actualize coroutines.

• The import articulation, which is utilized to import modules whose capacities or factors can be utilized as a part of the present program.

• The print proclamation was changed to the print() work in Python 3.

Python does not bolster tail call advancement or top of the line continuations, and, as indicated by Guido van Rossum, it never will. Nonetheless, better support for coroutine-like usefulness is given in 2.5, by expanding Python's generators. Before 2.5, generators were lethargic iterators; data was passed unidirectionally out of the generator. As of Python 2.5, it is conceivable to pass data over into a generator work, and as of Python 3.3, the data can be gone through various stack levels.

Expressions

Some Python expressions are like dialects, for example, C and Java, while some are most certainly not:

• Addition, subtraction, and duplication are the same, yet the conduct of division contrasts (see Mathematics for subtle elements). Python additionally included the ** administrator for exponentiation.

• As of Python 3.5, it bolsters framework augmentation specifically with the @ administrator, versus C and Java, which actualize these as library capacities. Prior forms of Python likewise utilized strategies rather than an infix administrator.

• In Python, == analyzes by esteem, versus Java, which looks at numerics by esteem and protests by reference. (Esteem correlations in Java on items can be performed with the equivalents() strategy.) Python's is administrator might be utilized to think about protest personalities (examination by reference). In Python, correlations might be binded, for instance a <= b <= c.

• Python utilizes the words and, or, not for its boolean administrators as opposed to the typical &&, ||, ! utilized as a part of Java and C.

• Python has a kind of expression named a rundown appreciation. Python 2.4 augmented rundown cognizances into a more broad expression named a generator expression.

• Anonymous capacities are actualized utilizing lambda expressions; nonetheless, these are constrained in that the body must be one expression.

• Conditional expressions in Python are composed as x if c else y (distinctive all together of operands from the c ? x : y administrator regular to numerous different dialects).

• Python makes a qualification amongst records and tuples. Records are composed as [1, 2, 3], are variable, and can't be utilized as the keys of lexicons (word reference keys must be permanent in Python). Tuples are composed as (1, 2, 3), are changeless and subsequently can be utilized as the keys of lexicons, gave all components of the tuple are permanent. The brackets around the tuple are discretionary in a few settings. Tuples can show up on the left half of an equivalent sign; subsequently an announcement like x, y = y, x can be utilized to swap two factors.

- Python has a "string design" administrator %. This capacities closely resembling printf design strings in C, e.g. "spam=%s eggs=%d" % ("blah", 2) assesses to "spam=blah eggs=2". In Python 3 and 2.6+, this was supplemented by the organization() strategy for the str class, e.g. "spam={0} eggs={1}".format("blah", 2).

- Python has different sorts of string literals:

o Strings delimited by single or twofold quote marks. Not at all like in Unix shells, Perl and Perl-affected dialects, single quote checks and twofold quote marks work indistinguishably. Both sorts of string utilize the oblique punctuation line (\) as an escape character and there is no understood string insertion, for example, "$spam".

o Triple-cited strings, which start and end with a progression of three single or twofold quote marks. They may traverse various lines and capacity like here archives in shells, Perl and Ruby.

o Raw string assortments, meant by prefixing the string exacting with a r. No escape groupings are deciphered; subsequently crude strings are valuable where strict oblique punctuation lines are normal, for example, customary expressions and Windows-style ways. Analyze "@-citing" in C#.

• Python has cluster file and exhibit cutting expressions on records, signified as a[key], a[start:stop] or a[start:stop:step]. Files are zero-based, and negative files are in respect to the end. Cuts take components from the begin record up to, yet excluding, the stop list. The third cut parameter, called step or walk, permits components to be skipped and switched. Cut files might be precluded, for instance a[:] gives back a duplicate of the whole rundown. Every component of a cut is a shallow duplicate.

In Python, a refinement amongst expressions and explanations is inflexibly authorized, rather than dialects, for example, Common Lisp, Scheme, or Ruby. This prompts to copying some usefulness. For instance:

• List appreciations versus for-circles

• Conditional expressions versus in the event that squares

• The eval() versus executive() worked in capacities (in Python 2, executive is an announcement); the previous is for expressions, the last is for articulations.

Articulations can't be a part of an expression, so list and different perceptions or lambda expressions, all being expressions, can't contain explanations. A specific instance of this is a task explanation, for example, a = 1 can't shape part of the restrictive articulation of a contingent proclamation. This has the benefit of evading a great C blunder of mixing up a task administrator = for an equity administrator == in conditions: if (c = 1) { ... } is grammatically legitimate (yet likely unintended) C code yet in the event that c = 1: ... causes a sentence structure mistake in Python.

Chapter 3

Techniques

Techniques on items are capacities appended to the question's class; the linguistic structure instance.method(argument) is, for ordinary strategies and capacities, syntactic sugar for Class.method(instance, contention). Python techniques have an unequivocal self parameter to get to example information, rather than the certain self (or this) in some other question situated programming dialects (e.g., C++, Java, Objective-C, or Ruby).

Writing

Python utilizes duck writing and has written questions yet untyped variable names. Sort limitations are not checked at aggregate time; rather, operations on a question may come up short, meaning that the given protest is not of an appropriate sort. In spite of being powerfully written, Python is specifically, restricting operations that are not very much characterized (for instance, adding a number to a string) as opposed to *q*uietly endeavoring to understand them.

Python permits software engineers to characterize their own particular sorts utilizing classes, which are regularly utilized for protest situated programming. New occasions of classes are built by calling the class (for instance, SpamClass() or EggsClass()), and the classes are examples of the metaclass sort (itself an occurrence of itself), permitting metaprogramming and reflection.

Before adaptation 3.0, Python had two sorts of classes: old-style and new-style. Old-style classes were disposed of in Python 3.0, making all classes new-style. In adaptations somewhere around 2.2 and 3.0, both sorts of classes could be utilized. The punctuation of both styles is the same, the distinction being whether the class *q*uestion is ac*q*uired from, specifically or by implication (all new-style classes acquire from protest and are occasions of sort).

Outline of Python 3's implicit sorts

Type Mutable Description Syntax case

str Immutable

A character string: grouping of Unicode codepoints 'Wikipedia'

"Wikipedia"

"""Traversing

various

lines"""

bytearray Mutable Sequence of bytes

bytearray(b'Some ASCII')

bytearray(b"Some ASCII")

bytearray([119, 105, 107, 105])

bytes Immutable Sequence of bytes
b'Some ASCII'

b"Some ASCII"

bytes([119, 105, 107, 105])

list Mutable List, can contain blended sorts

[4.0, 'string', True]

tuple Immutable Can contain blended types (4.0, 'string', True)

set Mutable Unordered set, contains no copies; can contain blended sorts if hashable {4.0, 'string', True}

frozenset Immutable Unordered set, contains no copies; can contain blended sorts if hashable frozenset([4.0, 'string', True])

dict Mutable Associative cluster (or word reference) of key and esteem sets; can contain blended sorts (keys and values), keys must be a hashable type {'key1': 1.0, 3: False}

int Immutable Integer of boundless greatness

float Immutable Floating point number, framework characterized accuracy

3.1415927

complex Immutable Complex number with genuine and nonexistent parts

3+2.7j

bool Immutable Boolean esteem

Genuine

False

ellipsis An ellipsis placeholder to be utilized as a file as a part of NumPy exhibits

...

Science

Python has the standard C number juggling administrators (+, - , *,/, %). It likewise has ** for exponentiation, e.g. 5**3 == 125 and 9**0.5 == 3.0, and another grid duplicate @ administrator is incorporated into variant 3.5.

The conduct of division has changed altogether after some time:

- Python 2.1 and prior utilize the C division conduct. The/administrator is number division if both operands are whole numbers, and skimming point division generally. Whole number division rounds towards 0, e.g. 7/3 == 2 and - 7/3 == - 2.

- Python 2.2 changes whole number division to round towards negative endlessness, e.g. 7/3 == 2 and - 7/3 == - 3. The floor division/administrator is presented. So 7/3 == 2, - 7/3 == - 3, 7.5/3 == 2.0 and - 7.5/3 == - 3.0. Including from _future_ import division causes a module to utilize Python 3.0 tenets for division (see next).

• Python 3.0 changes/to be continually skimming point division. In Python terms, the pre-3.0/is exemplary division, the adaptation 3.0/is genuine division, and/is floor division.

Adjusting towards negative vastness, however not the same as most dialects, includes consistency. For example, it implies that the condition (a+b)/b == a/b + 1 is constantly valid. It additionally implies that the condition b * (a/b) + a % b == an is substantial for both positive and negative estimations of a. In any case, keeping up the legitimacy of this condition implies that while the aftereffect of a % b is, obviously, in the half-open interim [0, b), where b is a positive number, it needs to lie in the interim (b, 0] when b is negative.

Python gives a round capacity to adjusting a buoy to the closest whole number. For tie-breaking, forms before 3 use round-far from zero: round(0.5) is 1.0, cycle(- 0.5) is −1.0. Python 3 utilizes round to even: round(1.5) is 2, round(2.5) is 2.

Python permits boolean expressions with numerous correspondence relations in a way that is steady with general use in science. For instance, the expression a < b < c tests whether an is not as much as b and b is not as much as c. C-inferred dialects translate this expression in an unexpected way: in C, the expression would first assess a < b, bringing about 0 or 1, and that outcome would then be contrasted and c.

Python has broad inherent support for self-assertive exactness number juggling. Whole numbers are straightforwardly changed from the machine-bolstered most extreme settled exactness (normally 32 or 64 bits), having a place with the python sort int, to self-assertive accuracy, having a place with the python sort long, where required. The last have a "L" addition in their literary representation. The Decimal sort/class in module decimal (since form 2.4) gives decimal skimming direct numbers toward discretionary exactness and a few adjusting modes. The Fraction sort in module portions (since adaptation 2.6) gives self-assertive exactness to levelheaded numbers.

Because of Python's broad science library, it is much of the time utilized as a logical scripting dialect to help in issues, for example, numerical information preparing and control.

Libraries

Python has a huge standard library, usually refered to as one of Python's most noteworthy qualities, giving instruments suited to many undertakings. This is consider and has been portrayed as a "batteries included" Python rationality. For Internet-confronting applications, numerous standard configurations and conventions, (for example, MIME and HTTP) are upheld. Modules for making graphical UIs, interfacing with social databases, pseudorandom number generators, math with subjective exactness decimals, controlling standard expressions, and doing unit testing are likewise included.

A few sections of the standard library are secured by particulars (for instance, the Web Server Gateway Interface (WSGI) execution wsgiref takes after PEP 333), however most modules are definitely not. They are indicated by their code, inner documentation, and test suite (if provided). Be that as it may, in light of the fact that a large portion of the standard library is cross-stage Python code, just a couple of modules need modifying or revising for variation usage.

The standard library is not expected to run Python or install it in an application. For instance, Blender 2.49 overlooks the vast majority of the standard library.

As of November, 2016, the Python Package Index, the official vault containing outsider programming for Python, contains more than 92,000 bundles offering an extensive variety of usefulness, including:

• graphical UIs, web systems, media, databases, systems administration and correspondences

• test structures, robotization and web scratching, documentation instruments, framework organization

• scientific figuring, content preparing, picture handling

Chapter 4

Improvement situations

Examination of coordinated advancement situations § Python

Most Python usage (counting CPython) can work as a summon line translator, for which the client enters articulations consecutively and gets the outcomes instantly (read–eval–print circle (REPL)). To put it plainly, Python goes about as a charge line interface or shell.

Different shells include capacities past those in the fundamental translator, including IDLE and IPython. While for the most part taking after the visual style of the Python shell, they execute highlights like auto-consummation, session state maintenance, and linguistic structure highlighting.

Notwithstanding standard desktop incorporated advancement situations (Python IDEs), there are additionally web program based IDEs, SageMath (proposed for creating science and math-related Python programs), and a program based IDE and facilitating environment, PythonAnywhere. Furthermore, the Canopy IDE is additionally a possibility for making programs written in Python.

Executions

Rundown of Python programming § Python executions

The primary Python execution, named CPython, is composed in C meeting the C89 standard. It aggregates Python programs into transitional bytecode, which is executed by the virtual machine. CPython is disseminated with an extensive standard library written in a blend of C and Python. It is accessible in adaptations for some stages, including Windows and most current Unix-like frameworks. CPython was planned from nearly its extremely origination to be cross-stage.

PyPy is a *q*uick, agreeable mediator of Python 2.7 and 3.2. Its in the nick of time compiler brings a huge speed change over CPython. A rendition exploiting multi-center processors utilizing programming value-based memory is being made.

Stackless Python is a critical fork of CPython that actualizes microthreads; it doesn't utilize the C memory stack, hence permitting enormously simultaneous projects. PyPy additionally has a stackless adaptation.

MicroPython is an incline, *q*uick Python 3 variation that is advanced to keep running on microcontrollers.

Other in the nick of time compilers have been produced before, however are presently unsupported:

• Google started a venture named Unladen Swallow in 2009 with the points of accelerating the Python mediator by 5 times, by utilizing the LLVM, and of enhancing its multithreading capacity to scale to a large number of centers.

• Psyco is an in the nick of time practicing compiler that incorporates with CPython and changes bytecode to machine code at runtime. The radiated code is specific for specific information sorts and is speedier than standard Python code.

In 2005, Nokia discharged a Python mediator for the Series 60 cell phones named PyS60. It incorporates a large portion of the modules from the CPython usage and some additional modules to coordinate with the Symbian working framework. This venture has been stayed up with the latest to keep running on all variations of the S60 stage and there are a few outsider modules accessible. The Nokia N900 additionally bolsters Python with GTK gadget libraries, with the element that projects can be both composed and keep running on the objective gadget.

There are a few compilers to abnormal state *q*uestion dialects, with either unlimited Python, a limited subset of Python, or a dialect like Python as the source dialect:

• Jython accumulates into Java byte code, which can then be executed by each Java virtual machine usage. This likewise empowers the utilization of Java class library capacities from the Python program.

• IronPython takes after a comparable approach keeping in mind the end goal to run Python programs on the .NET Common Language Runtime.

• The RPython dialect can be gathered to C, Java bytecode, or Common Intermediate Language, and is utilized to construct the PyPy mediator of Python.

• Pyjamas gathers Python to JavaScript.

• Shed Skin gathers Python to C++.

• Cython and Pyrex gather to C.

An execution correlation of different Python usage on a non-numerical (combinatorial) workload was displayed at EuroSciPy '13.

Advancement

Python's advancement is led generally through the Python Enhancement Proposal (PEP) handle. The PEP procedure is the essential instrument for proposing major new elements, for gathering group contribution on an issue, and for recording the plan choices that have gone into Python. Extraordinary PEPs are looked into and remarked upon by the Python people group and by Van

Rossum, the Python venture's kindhearted despot forever.

Improvement of the dialect obliges advancement of the CPython reference usage. The mailing list python-dev is the essential gathering for dialog about the dialect's advancement; particular issues are examined in the Roundup bug tracker kept up at python.org. Advancement happens on a self-facilitated source code store running Mercurial.

CPython's open discharges come in three sorts, recognized by which part of the variant number is increased:

• Backwards-inconsistent renditions, where code is relied upon to break and should be physically ported. The initial segment of the form number is augmented. These discharges happen occasionally—for instance, form 3.0 was discharged 8 years after 2.0.

• Major or "highlight" discharges, which are generally good yet present new elements. The second part of the rendition number is increased. These discharges are booked to happen generally like clockwork, and every significant rendition is bolstered by bugfixes for quite a while after its discharge.

• Bugfix discharges, which present no new components yet settle bugs. The third and last part of the variant number is increased. These discharges are made at whatever point an adequate number of bugs have been settled upstream since the last discharge, or generally at regular intervals. Security vulnerabilities are likewise fixed in bugfix discharges.

Numerous alpha, beta, and discharge competitors are additionally discharged as sneak peaks, and for testing before conclusive discharges. In spite of the fact that there is an unpleasant timetable for every discharge, this is regularly pushed back if the code is not prepared. The advancement group screens the condition of the code by running the extensive unit test suite amid improvement, and utilizing the BuildBot persistent mix framework.

The people group of Python designers has additionally contributed more than 86,000 programming modules (as of August 20, 2016) to the Python Package Index (PyPI), the official storehouse of outsider libraries for Python.

The significant scholastic meeting on Python is named PyCon. There are extraordinary tutoring programs like the Pyladies.

Naming

Python's name is gotten from the TV arrangement Monty Python's Flying Circus, and it is normal to utilize Monty Python references in illustration code. For instance, the metasyntactic factors regularly utilized as a part of Python writing are spam and eggs, rather than the conventional foo and bar. Likewise, the official Python documentation frequently contains different cloud Monty Python references.

The prefix Py-is utilized to demonstrate that something is identified with Python. Cases of the utilization of this prefix in names of Python applications or libraries incorporate Pygame, an authoritative of SDL to Python (generally used to make diversions); PyS60, an execution for the Symbian S60 working framework; PyQt and PyGTK, which tie Qt and GTK, separately, to Python; and PyPy, a Python usage initially written in Python.

Employments

Chapter 5

List of Python programming

Since 2003, Python has reliably positioned in the main ten most prevalent programming dialects as measured by the TIOBE Programming Community Index. As of August 2016, it is the fifth most prevalent dialect. It was positioned as Programming Language of the Year for the year 2007 and 2010. It is the third most prevalent dialect whose linguistic sentence structure is not overwhelmingly in light of C, e.g. C++, Objective-C (note, C# and Java just have fractional syntactic likeness to C, for example, the utilization of wavy props, and are nearer in similitude to each other than C).

An exact review discovered scripting dialects, (for example, Python) more profitable than traditional dialects, (for example, C and Java) for a programming issue including string control and hunt in a word reference. Memory utilization was regularly "superior to Java and very little more regrettable than C or C++".

Expansive associations that make utilization of Python incorporate Wikipedia, Google, Yahoo!, CERN, NASA, and some littler ones like ILM, and ITA. The social news organizing site, Reddit, is composed completely in Python.

Python can serve as a scripting dialect for web applications, e.g., by means of mod_wsgi for the Apache web server. With Web Server Gateway Interface, a standard API has advanced to encourage these applications. Web systems like Django, Pylons, Pyramid, TurboGears, web2py, Tornado, Flask, Bottle and Zope bolster engineers in the plan and support of complex applications. Night wear and IronPython can be utilized to build up the customer side of Ajax-based applications. SQLAlchemy can be utilized as information mapper to a social database. Turned is a system to program correspondences amongst PCs, and is utilized (for instance) by Dropbox.

Libraries like NumPy, SciPy and Matplotlib permit the viable utilization of Python in logical registering, with particular libraries, for example, Biopython and Astropy giving space particular usefulness. SageMath is a scientific programming with a "scratch pad" programmable in Python: its library covers numerous parts of arithmetic, including variable based math, combinatorics, numerical science, number hypothesis, and analytics. The Python dialect re-executed in Java stage is utilized for numeric and measurable estimations with 2D/3D representation by the DMelt extend.

Python has been effectively implanted in numerous product items as a scripting dialect, incorporating into limited component strategy programming, for example, Abaqus, 3D parametric modeler like FreeCAD, 3D liveliness bundles, for example, 3ds Max, Blender, Cinema 4D, Lightwave, Houdini, Maya, modo, MotionBuilder, Softimage, the visual impacts printer Nuke, 2D imaging programs like GIMP, Inkscape, Scribus and Paint Shop Pro, and melodic documentation program or scorewriter capella. GNU Debugger utilizes Python as a beautiful printer to show complex structures, for example, C++ holders. Esri advances Python as the best decision for composing scripts in ArcGIS. It has likewise been utilized as a part of a few computer games, and has been received as first of the three accessible programming dialects in Google App Engine, the other two being Java and Go. Python is likewise utilized as a part of algorithmic exchanging and quantitative back. Python can likewise be executed in APIs of online financiers that keep running on different dialects by utilizing wrappers.

Python has been utilized as a part of manmade brainpower assignments. As a scripting dialect with module engineering, straightforward linguistic structure and rich content handling apparatuses, Python is frequently utilized for normal dialect preparing assignments.

Many working frameworks incorporate Python as a standard segment; the dialect ships with most Linux disseminations,

AmigaOS 4, FreeBSD, NetBSD, OpenBSD and OS X, and can be utilized from the terminal. Numerous Linux conveyances utilize installers written in Python: Ubuntu utilizes the Ubiquity installer, while Red Hat Linux and Fedora utilize the Anaconda installer. Gentoo Linux utilizes Python as a part of its bundle administration framework, Portage.

Python has likewise observed broad use in the data security industry, incorporating into endeavor advancement.

The vast majority of the Sugar programming for the One Laptop for every Child XO, now created at Sugar Labs, is composed in Python.

The Raspberry Pi single-board PC extend has embraced Python as its principle client programming dialect.

LibreOffice incorporates Python and means to supplant Java with Python. Python Scripting Provider is a center component since Version 4.0 from 7 February 2013.

Dialects affected by Python

Python's plan and reasoning have impacted a few programming dialects, including:

• Boo utilizes space, a comparable punctuation, and a comparative protest show. In any case, Boo utilizes static writing (and discretionary duck writing) and is firmly incorporated with the .NET Framework.

• Cobra utilizes space and a comparative sentence structure. Cobra's "Affirmations" archive records Python first among dialects that impacted it. Be that as it may, Cobra straightforwardly underpins configuration by-contract, unit tests, and discretionary static writing.

• ECMAScript acquired iterators, generators, and rundown understandings from Python.

• Go is depicted as fusing the "advancement speed of working in a dynamic dialect like Python".

• Groovy was inspired by the longing to convey the Python outline logic to Java.

• Julia was outlined "with genuine macros [.. what's more, to be] as usable for general programming as Python [and] ought to be as quick as C". Calling to or from Julia is conceivable; to with PyCall.jl and a Python bundle pyjulia permits calling, in the other course, from Python.

- OCaml has a discretionary sentence structure, named twt (The Whitespace Thing), motivated by Python and Haskell.

- Ruby's maker, Yukihiro Matsumoto, has said: "I needed a scripting dialect that was more capable than Perl, and more protest arranged than Python. That is the reason I chose to outline my own dialect."

- CoffeeScript is a programming dialect that cross-gathers to JavaScript; it has Python-enlivened language structure.

- Swift is a programming dialect imagined by Apple; it has some Python-enlivened language structure.

Python's advancement rehearses have likewise been copied by different dialects. The act of requiring a record portraying the method of reasoning for, and issues encompassing, a change to the dialect (for Python's situation, a PEP) is additionally utilized as a part of Tcl and Erlang due to Python's impact.

Python has been granted a TIOBE Programming Language of the Year grant twice (in 2007 and 2010), which is given to the dialect with the best development in notoriety through the span of a year.

5 Compelling Reasons to Learn Python as Your First Programming Language

We've all heard the exhortation: school will furnish us with the apparatuses we have to succeed, and advanced education will be the steed that will convey us over the foggy fields of work towards our fantasy. Rather, we find to our terrify that our heavenly steed is only a man strolling behind us, crashing two coconuts together. More regrettable, we locate a self-trained programming engineer walk by, the splendid standards of his million-dollar startup waving in his trail. Turns out that while we squandered our time wheeling and dealing for gourds (read: lessening work opportunities and measly compensations), he has shown himself three programming dialects, abandoning us wishing we did likewise.

All things considered, it's never past the point of no return. You're never excessively old nor excessively youthful, making it impossible, making it impossible to begin figuring out how to program. Where to begin? We recommend beginning with Python, whose namesake — in the event that you haven't speculated as of now — is propelled by the British comic drama gather Monty Python. So what would it be a good idea for you to anticipate from a PC programming dialect named after a gathering that ridicules pretty much everything? All things considered, there's a glaring hint some place yet we'll give you five convincing reasons why Python ought to be your first raid into programming.

5 Reasons You Should Learn Python First:

1. Simple to-Learn

Let's be honest. Taking in a programming dialect doesn't sound as energizing as a breakdance rivalry on a plane carrying warship. Fortunately, Python was planned on account of the newcomer. Python peruses like kindergarten math and is simple on the layman's eye. The utilization of white space and regular expressions has wiped out the requirement for repetitive variable announcements and ugly wavy sections. Python likewise requires less code to finish essential errands, making it a conservative dialect to learn. Python code is regularly 3-5 times shorter than Java, and 5-10 times shorter than C++. Be that as it may, while Python is anything but difficult to learn in itself, we as a whole know the hazard of concentrate alone and ill-equipped. Homer Simpson did that in school and look where it got him. Luckily, the Python people group has amassed a sufficient gathering of assets to keep you protected and beneficial.

The acclaimed satire troupe Monty Python likewise enlivened the name of the Python programming dialect.

2. You're Stepping Stone

Python can be your venturing stone into the programming universe. Managers are searching for completely stacked developers and Python will help you arrive. Python is a *q*uestion situated dialect, much the same as Javascript, C++, C#, Perl, Ruby, and other key programming dialects. For individuals wanting to wind up programming engineers, taking in this sort of programming in one region will help you adjust effortlessly in different situations.

In particular, a working information of Python can be a strong establishment since Python's strategies can be utilized as a part of an expansive scope of uses. For instance, Python's characteristic association and design can go about as your Rosetta Stone when attempting to decode more secretive programming dialects. Here's a brief examination of Python with two different dialects: Ruby and PHP. Ruby has a comparative structure to Python while PHP has an altogether different language structure.

A "for" circle on a rundown [Python]:

An "every" call with a square on an exhibit [Ruby]:

A "while" circle in Python:

A "while" circle in PHP:

Without earlier programming knowledge, anybody can undoubtedly recognize the likenesses and contrasts between Python's grammar and those of different dialects. In any case, an essential comprehension of Python makes hopping into Ruby a breeze, while unraveling a PHP code turns into a simpler undertaking. When you take in the Zen of Python you can utilize it to help you prevail with regards to creating code in any dialect.

Move into overdrive with these top prescribed courses.

3. What about Some Raspberry Pi?

Making programming fun is no simple undertaking, whether your understudies are learners, prepared veterans, or youngsters. Hell, even the most eager instructors battle to get anybody amped up for composing code. However, marvels do happen occasionally: overcoming any issues between dynamic registering and genuine applications is currently as simple as Pi.

Raspberry Pi is a card-sized, reasonable microcomputer that is being utilized for an astounding scope of energizing do-it-without anyone's help stuff, for example, robots, remote-controlled autos, and computer game consoles. With Python as its fundamental programming dialect, the Raspberry Pi is being utilized even by children to assemble radios, cameras, arcade machines, and pet feeders! With Raspberry Pi insanity on the uptrend, there are endless DIY activities, instructional exercises, and books to look over on the web. These will help you fan out from your "welcome world" starter projects to something you can genuinely be glad for. While you won't develop a small scale Voltron at any point in the near future, the feeling of fulfillment you'll get from finishing one of these DIY tasks will propel you to drive yourself more remote than computerizing an ASCII tic-tac-toe diversion.

4. Cash Money

On the off chance that planning a talking skull that sings arbitrary tweets from Gary Busey utilizing Python and Raspberry Pi isn't a sufficiently major motivator, then what about the possibility of having a much fatter wallet? Organizations, for example, Google, Yahoo!, Disney, Nokia, and IBM all utilization Python. Truth be told, among programming dialects, Python had the biggest year-on-year work request development — at 19% — as of March 2013. Quite, the general enlisting interest for IT experts plunged year over year by 5% as of January 2014, aside from Python developers which expanded by 8.7%. In New York, Python engineers positioned

#8 of the most popular tech laborers, making a normal of $106k/year. On the opposite side of the Atlantic, Python software engineers additionally appreciate an emphatically rising interest for their aptitudes as appeared by the accompanying diagram.

Source1

5. It Works Online Too

Web advancement is still a blasting monetary prospect for developers. With Python's immeasurable abilities, you also can have a slice of the profits. Django — the well known open source web application system written in Python — is the establishment of such locales as Pinterest, The New York Times, The Guardian, Bit Bucket, and Instagram. Django is a total structure that removes the multifaceted nature from web improvement while as yet giving you control over as much as you need. As an open-source system, all the data you have to begin can be found at DjangoProject.com.

Python is the main scripting dialect you'll have to start outlining your own particular sites and applications. What's valid with Python is valid with Django. Web advancement with Django is very much recorded, has an extensive bolster group, and takes less time and code. With Django, awesome thoughts can crystalize speedier as their advancement requires less engineers and less scripting hours on the console. This will give you more opportunity to improve your ideas and transform them into expert review items. Of course, Django isn't the main quick improvement structure worked for Python developers. There are a lot of light weight and full stacked alternatives that you can investigate.

Why Python?

My first take a gander at Python was a mishap, and I didn't much like what I saw at the time. It was mid 1997, and Mark Lutz's book Programming Python from O'Reilly and Associates had as of late turned out. O'Reilly books once in a while arrive on my doorstep, chose from among the new discharges by some secretive advocate inside the association utilizing an arbitrary procedure I've surrendered attempting to get it.

One of them was Programming Python. I discovered this to some degree fascinating, as I gather scripts. I know more than two dozen broadly useful dialects, compose compilers and translators for no particular reason, and have outlined any number of uncommon reason dialects and markup formalisms myself. My most as of late finished venture, as I compose this, is an extraordinary reason dialect called SNG for controlling PNG (Portable Network Graphics) pictures.

I had effectively heard quite recently enough about Python to realize that it is what is these days called a "scripting dialect", an interpretive dialect with its own particular inherent memory administration and great offices for calling and coordinating with different projects. So I jumped into Programming Python with one question highest in my brain: what has this understood Perl does not?

Perl, obviously, is the 800-pound gorilla of cutting edge scripting dialects. It has to a great extent supplanted shell as the scripting dialect of decision for framework executives, on account of its far reaching set of UNIX library and framework calls, and somewhat to the immense gathering of Perl modules worked by an exceptionally dynamic Perl people group. The dialect is normally evaluated to be the CGI dialect behind around 85% of the "live" substance on the Net. Larry Wall, its maker, is properly viewed as a standout amongst the most essential pioneers in the Open Source people group, and regularly positions third behind Linus Torvalds and Richard Stallman in the present pantheon of programmer demigods.

Around then, I had utilized Perl for various little undertakings. I'd discovered it very intense, regardless of the possibility that the linguistic structure and some different parts of the dialect appeared to be somewhat impromptu and inclined to chomp one if not utilized with care. I couldn't help suspecting that Python would have a significant slope to move up 'til now another scripting dialect, so as I read, I searched first for what appeared to separate it from Perl.

I promptly stumbled over the principal odd component of Python that everybody sees: the way that whitespace (space) is really critical in the dialect linguistic structure. The dialect has no simple of the C and Perl support punctuation; rather, changes in space delimit explanation bunches. Also, as most programmers on first understanding this reality, I pulled back in reflexive nauseate.

I am scarcely mature enough to have modified in group FORTRAN for a couple of months back in the 1970s. Most programmers aren't nowadays, however some way or another our way of life appears to have held an entirely exact society memory of how frightful those old-style settled field dialects were. Without a doubt, the expression "free configuration", utilized in those days to depict the more current style of token-situated punctuation in Pascal and C, has nearly been overlooked; the sum total of what dialects have been planned that path throughout recent decades. Alternately all, in any case. It's difficult to accuse anybody, on observing this Python include, for at first responding just as they had suddenly ventured in a steaming heap of dinosaur compost.

That is unquestionably how I felt. I skimmed through whatever is left of the dialect depiction without much intrigue. I didn't see much else to prescribe Python, aside from perhaps that the punctuation appeared to be preferably cleaner than Perl's and the offices for doing essential GUI components like catches and menus looked genuinely great.

I set the book back on the rack, giving careful consideration that I ought to code some sort of little GUI-focused venture in Python at some point, just to ensure I truly comprehended the dialect. Be that as it may, I didn't accept what I'd seen could ever contend successfully with Perl.

A ton of different things planned to hold that note path down on my need list for a long time. Whatever remains of 1997 was momentous for me; it was, in addition to other things, the year I composed and distributed the first form of "The Cathedral and the Bazaar". Be that as it may, I found time to compose a few Perl programs, including two of critical size and intricacy. One of them, attendant, is the right hand still used to document approaching entries at the Metalab programming file. The other, anthologize, was utilized to naturally produce the PostScript for the 6th release of Linux from the Linux Documentation Project's file of HOWTOs. Both projects are accessible at Metalab.

Composing these projects left me continuously less happy with Perl. Bigger venture measure appeared to amplify some of Perl's inconveniences into genuine, proceeding with issues. The language structure that had appeared to be only offbeat at a hundred lines started to appear like a near invulnerable fence of thistles at a thousand. "More than one approach to do it" loaned flavor and expressiveness at a little scale, however made it fundamentally harder to keep up reliable style over a more extensive code base. Furthermore, a significant number of the elements that were later fixed into Perl to address the intricacy control needs of greater projects (objects, lexical checking, "utilize strict", and so on.) had a delicate, jerry-fixed feel about them.

These issues joined to make vast volumes of Perl code appear to be preposterously hard to peruse and get a handle on all in all after just a couple days' nonattendance. Additionally, I discovered I was investing increasingly energy grappling with antiquities of the dialect as opposed to my application issues. What's more, most cursing of all, the subsequent code was terrible—this matters. Appalling projects resemble monstrous suspension scaffolds: they're significantly more at risk to crumple than truly ones, on the grounds that the way people (particularly build people) see excellence is personally identified with our capacity to handle and comprehend unpredictability. A dialect that makes it difficult to compose ex*q*uisite code makes it difficult to compose great code.

With a pattern of two dozen dialects added to my repertoire, I could distinguish all the indications of a dialect plan that had been pushed to the edge of its utilitarian envelope. By mid-1997, I was considering "there must be a superior way" and started throwing about for a more rich scripting dialect.

One course I didn't consider was retreating to C as a default dialect. The days when it appeared well and good to do your own memory administration in another program are long over, outside of a couple forte ranges like part hacking, logical figuring and 3-D design—places where you completely should get most extreme speed and tight control of memory use, since you have to push the e*q*uipment as hard as could be expected under the circumstances.

For most different circumstances, tolerating the investigating overhead of cushion overwhelms, pointer-associating issues, malloc/free memory breaks and the various related ills is only insane on today's machines. Far superior to exchange a couple cycles and a couple of kilobytes of memory for the overhead of a scripting dialect's memory chief and manage on much more profitable human time. Without a doubt, the benefits of this methodology are definitely what has driven the hazardous development of Perl since the mid-1990s.

I played with Tcl, just to find rapidly that it scales up significantly more inadequately than Perl. Old LISPer that I am, I additionally took a gander at different current lingos of Lisp and Scheme—at the same time, as is generally normal for Lisp, bunches of astute outline was rendered practically futile by inadequate or nonexistent documentation, deficient access to POSIX/UNIX offices, and a little however all things considered profoundly divided client group. Perl's ubiquity is not a mishap; the vast majority of its rivals are either more regrettable than Perl for extensive activities or by one means or another no place close as helpful as their hypothetically better outlines should than make them.

My second take a gander at Python was nearly as unplanned as my first. In October 1997, a progression of inquiries on the fetchmail-companions mailing list made it clear that end clients were experiencing expanding difficulty creating arrangement documents for my fetchmail utility. The record utilizes a straightforward, traditionally UNIX free-organize sentence structure, yet can turn out to be forbiddingly muddled when a client has POP3 and IMAP accounts at various locales. For instance, see Listing 1 for a to some degree streamlined adaptation of mine.

Posting 1

I chose to assault the issue by composing an end-easy to understand design editorial manager, fetchmailconf. The plan target of fetchmailconf was clear: to totally conceal the control record language structure behind an elegant, ergonomically revise GUI interface loaded with choice catches, slider bars and round out structures.

The prospect of actualizing this in Perl did not excite me. I had seen GUI code in Perl, and it was a spiky blend of Perl and Tcl that looked considerably uglier than my own particular unadulterated Perl code. It was now I recollected the bit I had set over six months before. This could be a chance to get a few hands-on involvement with Python.

Obviously, this conveyed me eye to eye at the end of the day with Python's pons asinorum, the noteworthiness of whitespace. This time, be that as it may, I charged ahead and roughed out some code for a modest bunch of test GUI components. Strangely, Python's utilization of whitespace quit feeling unnatural after around twenty minutes. I just indented code, practically as I would have done in a C program at any rate, and it worked.

That was my first astonish. My second came a few hours into the venture, when I saw (considering delays expected to look into new elements in Programming Python) I was creating working code almost as *q*uick as I could sort. When I understood this, I was very startled. An imperative measure of exertion in coding is the recurrence with which you compose something that doesn't really coordinate your mental representation of the issue, and need to backtrack on understanding that what you just wrote won't really advise the dialect to do what you're considering. A critical measure of good dialect configuration is the manner by which *q*uickly the rate of stumbles of this kind falls as you pick up involvement with the dialect.

When you're composing working code almost as *q*uick as you can sort and your slip rate is close to zero, it by and large means you've accomplished authority of the dialect. In any case, that didn't bode well, since it was still the very beginning and I was fre*q*uently delaying to look into new dialect and library highlights!

This was my first piece of information that, in Python, I was really managing a particularly decent outline. Most dialects have so much erosion and ungainliness incorporated with their plan that you learn a large portion of their list of capabilities much sooner than your slip rate drops anyplace close to zero. Python was the principal broadly useful dialect I'd ever utilized that turned around this procedure.

Not that it took me long to take in the list of capabilities. I composed a working, usable fetchmailconf, with GUI, in six working days, of which maybe what might as well be called two days were spent learning Python itself. This mirrors another helpful property of the dialect: it is conservative - you can hold its whole list of capabilities (and no less than an idea file of its libraries) in your mind. C is a broadly minimized dialect. Perl is famously not; something the idea "There's more than one approach to do it!" costs Perl is the likelihood of smallness.

Be that as it may, my most emotional snapshot of disclosure lay ahead. My plan had an issue: I could undoubtedly create arrangement records from the client's GUI activities, however altering them was a much more difficult issue. Then again, rather, understanding them into an editable shape was an issue.

The parser for fetchmail's setup record linguistic structure is somewhat intricate. It's really composed in YACC and Lex, two great UNIX apparatuses for creating dialect parsing code in C. With the goal for fetchmailconf to have the capacity to alter existing design documents, I thought it would need to duplicate that intricate parser in Python. I was extremely hesitant to do this, mostly in view of the measure of work included and incompletely on the grounds that I wasn't certain how to discover that two parsers in two unique dialects acknowledge the same. The exact opposite thing I required was the additional work of keeping the two parsers in synchronization as the setup dialect advanced!

This issue confused me for some time. At that point I had a motivation: I'd let fetchmailconf utilize fetchmail's own parser! I included a - configdump choice to fetchmail that would parse .fetchmailrc and dump the outcome to standard yield in the organization of a Python initializer. For the document over, the outcome would look generally like Listing 2 (to spare space, a few information not applicable to the case is overlooked).

Posting 2

Python could then assess the fetchmail - configdump yield and have the design accessible as the estimation of the variable "fetchmail".

This wasn't exactly the last stride in the move. What I truly needed wasn't only for fetchmailconf to have the current arrangement, however to transform it into a connected tree of live protests. There would be three sorts of articles in this tree: Configuration (the top-level protest speaking to the whole setup), Site (speaking to one of the locales to be surveyed) and User (speaking to client information connected to a site). The case record portrays five site protests, each with one client question connected to it.

I had effectively planned and composed the three protest classes (that is the thing that took four days, the greater part of it spent getting the design of the gadgets without flaw). Each had a technique that made it fly up a GUI alter board to adjust its occurrence information. My final issue was some way or another to change the dead information in this Python initializer into live questions.

I considered written work code that would unequivocally think about the structure of every one of the three classes and utilize that information to stoop through the initializer making coordinating items, however dismisses that thought in light of the fact that new class individuals were probably going to be included after some time as the setup dialect developed new components. In the event that I composed the question creation code in the undeniable way, it would be delicate and tend to drop out of synchronize when either the class definitions or the initializer structure changed.

What I truly needed was code that would break down the shape and individuals from the initializer, inquiry the class definitions themselves about their individuals, and afterward alter itself to impedance-coordinate the two sets.

This sort of thing is called metaclass hacking and is for the most part considered fearsomely recondite— profound dark enchantment. Most protest arranged dialects don't bolster it by any means; in those that do (Perl being one), it has a tendency to be a muddled and delicate undertaking. I had been inspired by Python's low coefficient of grinding as such, however here was a genuine test. How hard would I need to grapple with the dialect to motivate it? I knew from past experience that the session was probably going to be agonizing, notwithstanding accepting I won, however I plunged into the book and read up on Python's metaclass offices. The subsequent capacity is appeared in Listing 3, and the code that calls it is in Listing 4.

Posting 3

Posting 4

That doesn't search too terrible for profound dark enchantment, isn't that right? Thirty-two lines, tallying remarks. Just from realizing what I've said in regards to the class structure, the calling code is even decipherable. Be that as it may, the measure of this code isn't the genuine stunner. Prepare yourself: this code just took me around a hour and a half to compose—and it worked effectively the first occasion when I ran it.

To state I was dumbfounded would have been emphatically floundering in modest representation of the truth. It's sufficiently exceptional when executions of basic strategies work precisely not surprisingly the first run through; however my first metaclass hack in another dialect, six days from a cool standing begin? Regardless of the possibility that we stipulate that I am a genuinely skilled programmer, this is a stunning demonstration of Python's clarity and style of outline.

There was basically no chance I could have pulled off an overthrow like this in Perl, even with my endlessly more noteworthy experience level in that dialect. It was now I understood I was presumably deserting Perl.

This was my most sensational Python minute. Be that as it may, when all is said and done, it was only an astute hack. The long haul value of a dialect comes not in its capacity to bolster astute hacks, but rather from how well and how inconspicuously it underpins the everyday function of programming. The everyday work of programming comprises not of composing new projects, but rather generally perusing and altering existing ones.

So the genuine punchline of the story is this: weeks and months subsequent to composing fetchmailconf, I could at present read the fetchmailconf code and grok what it was managing without genuine mental exertion. Also, the genuine reason I no longer compose Perl for anything besides little activities is that was never genuine when I was composing substantial masses of Perl code. I fear the possibility of continually modifying manager or anthologize once more— however fetchmailconf gives me no apprehensions by any means.

Perl still has its employments. For minor ventures (100 lines or less) that include a great deal of content example coordinating, I am still more inclined to tinker up a Perl-regexp-based arrangement than to go after Python. For good late cases of such things, see the timeseries and growthplot scripts in the fetchmail appropriation. Really, these are much similar to the things Perl did in its unique part as a kind of blend awk/sed/grep/sh, before it had works and direct access to the working framework API. For anything bigger or more mind boggling, I have come to incline toward the unobtrusive excellencies of Python—and I think you will, as well.

What is Python Used For?

When I have to assemble a web application, I go after Python. When I have to computerize some little errand on my framework, I go after Python. When I need to locate the most widely recognized hues in a picture, I go after Python. When I... OK, I think you get the photo. Fundamentally, when I have to code something and the dialect doesn't make a difference, I utilize Python. So what is Python?

Python is a broadly useful programming dialect made in the late 1980s, and named after Monty Python, that is utilized by a great many individuals to get things done from testing microchips at Intel, to fueling Instagram, to building computer games with the PyGame library. It's little, nearly looks like the English dialect, and has several current outsider libraries.

So what are the significant reasons why I, for one, pick Python and prescribe it to whatever number individuals as could reasonably be expected? It boils down to three reasons.

Intelligibility

Python nearly looks like the English dialect, utilizing words like "not" and "in" to make it to where you can all the time read a program, or script, out loud to another person and not feel like you're talking some arcane dialect. This is likewise helped by Python's exceptionally strict accentuation rules which implies you don't have wavy supports ({ }) everywhere on your code.

Additionally, Python has an arrangement of guidelines, known as PEP 8, that advise each Python designer how to organize their code. This implies you generally know where to put new lines and, all the more vitally, that essentially every other Python script you get, whether it was composed by a beginner or a prepared proficient, will look fundamentally the same as and be similarly as simple to peruse. The way that my Python code, with five or so years of experience, looks fundamentally the same as the code that Guido van Rossum (the maker of Python) composes is such a sense of self support.

Libraries

Python has been around for more than 20 years, so a considerable measure of code written in Python has developed throughout the decades and, being an open source dialect, a great deal of this has been discharged for others to utilize. All of it is gathered, purported "pie-pee-eye" or, all the more regularly called "the CheeseShop". You can introduce this product on your framework to be utilized by your own particular tasks. For instance, in the event that you need to utilize Python to manufacture scripts with commandline contentions, you'd introduce the "snap" library and afterward import it into your scripts and utilize it. There are libraries for basically any utilization case you can think of, from picture control, to logical computations, to server computerization.

Group

Python has client amasses all over the place, more often than not called PUGs, and majors gatherings on each landmass other than Antarctica. PyCon NA, the biggest Python meeting in North America, sold out its 2,500 tickets this year. What's more, mirroring Python's dedication to differences, it had more than 30% ladies speakers. PyCon NA 2013 likewise began a pattern of offering "Youthful Coder" workshops, where participants instructed Python to kids somewhere around 9 and 16 years old for a day, getting them acquainted with the dialect and, at last, helping them hack and mod a few diversions on the Raspberry Pis they were given. Being a piece of a such a positive group does a considerable measure to keep you spurred.

I'm extremely eager to have the capacity to impart my most loved dialect to the

Treehouse people group and ideally the bits of Python that I adore the most will help you choose to look at it and learn it with me.

Conclusion

Thank you again for downloading this book!

I hope this book was able to help you have a clear insight about Python

Finally, if you enjoyed this book, then I'd like to ask you for a favor, would you be kind enough to leave a review for this book on Amazon? It'd be greatly appreciated!

Thank you and good luck!

I truly do appreciate it!

Best Wishes,

Lee Maxwell